THIS BOOK
BELONGS TO ~
....

All the World's a Stage

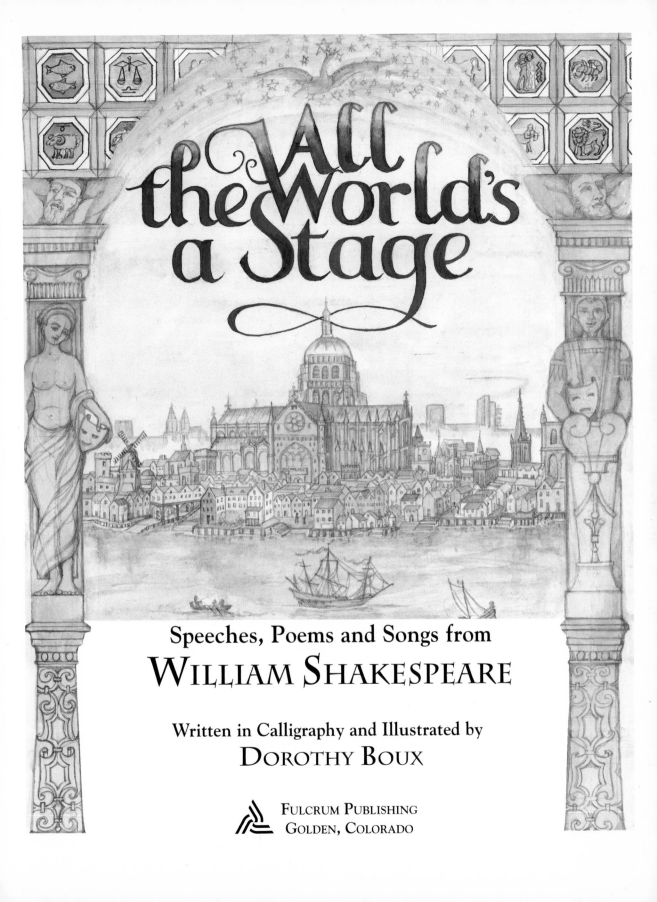

All the World's a Stage

Speeches, Poems and Songs from
WILLIAM SHAKESPEARE

Written in Calligraphy and Illustrated by
DOROTHY BOUX

FULCRUM PUBLISHING
GOLDEN, COLORADO

Copyright © 1996 Dorothy Boux
First U.S. publication October 1996
First published 1994 by Shepheard-Walwyn (Publishers) Ltd.
26 Charing Cross Road (Suite 34) London WC2H ODH
in association with
Ficino Press
84 High Street Harrow-on-the-Hill HA1 3LW
Book design by Dorothy Boux

Library of Congress Cataloging-in-Publication Data
Shakespeare. William, 1564-1616.
All the world's a stage: speeches, poems, and
songs from William Shakespeare/written in
calligraphy and illustrated by Dorothy Boux.
p. cm.
Includes index.
ISBN 1-55591-338-5 (hardcover)
1. Shakespeare, William, 1564-1616 -- Quotations.
2. Calligraphy--Specimens. 3. Quotations, English.
I. Boux, Dorothy. II. Title.
PR2892.B68 1996
822.3'3 -- dc20   96 -5767
                                            CIP
Printed and bound in Great Britain by BPC Books, Ltd.
0987654321
Fulcrum Publishing
350 Indiana Street, Suite 350
Golden, Colorado 80401-5093 U.S.A.
(800) 992-2908 * (303) 277-1623

TABLE OF CONTENTS

*What fairies haunt
this ground?
A book? O rare one!
Be not, as is our
fangled world, a
garment*

*Nobler than that it
covers: let thy effects
So follow, to be most
unlike our courtiers,
As good as promise.
Cymbeline.*

ACKNOWLEDGEMENTS

The calligrapher has used the text of the Oxford Shakespeare published in 1905 and edited by W. J. Craig, M.A.

During the course of this work there has been unfailing support and help from Peter Weigall, who first conceived the idea of presenting Shakespeare in calligraphy and illustration. He has helped with the selection of the contents, prepared the index, and composed the introductory texts. In short, he has undertaken the background work which is so essential, and thus released the calligrapher for other things. Our heartfelt thanks go to him.

ALL THE WORLD'S A STAGE

This tapestry of Shakespeare's words opens with Jaques' broad and humorous view of the stages of man's life, followed by a king musing on the measured, simple life of a shepherd, and the Archbishop's metaphor of the ordered beehive. Then the joy of the morning, the world of fairyland and the glorious presence of the goddesses follow. Turning to the affairs of the heart: Romeo adores Juliet, Viola advises on wooing, Speed describes the comic behaviour of lovers, Theseus compares the frenzy shared by the lunatic, the lover and the poet, and the voice of Shakespeare speaks of true love. In the fairy kingdom, Oberon interferes with the amorous affairs of others and makes his queen fall in love with an ass; and Queen Mab plays havoc with people's dreams.

All the world's a stage,
And all the men and women merely players;
They have their exits and their entrances,
And one man in his time plays many parts,
His acts being seven ages... At first the infant,
Mewling and puking in the nurse's arms:
Then the whining school-boy, with his satchel
And shining morning face, creeping like snail
Unwillingly to school: and then the lover,
Sighing like furnace, with a woeful ballad,
Made to his mistress' eyebrow: then a soldier,
Full of strange oaths and bearded like the pard,
Jealous in honour, sudden and quick in quarrel,
Seeking the bubble reputation
Even in the cannon's mouth: and then the justice,
In fair round belly with good capon lined,
With eyes severe and beard of formal cut,
Full of wise saws and modern instances,
And so he plays his part... The sixth age shifts
Into the lean and slippered pantaloon,
With spectacles on nose and pouch on side,
His youthful hose, well-saved, a world too wide
For his shrunk shank, and his big manly voice,
Turning again toward childish treble, pipes
And whistles in his sound... Last scene of all,
That ends this strange eventful history,
Is second childishness, and mere oblivion
Sans teeth, sans eyes, sans taste, sans everything.

As You Like It - Act II - Sc.7

O GOD !

methinks it were a happy
life,   To be no better than
a homely swain;   To sit upon
a hill, as I do now,   To carve
out dials quaintly, point to point,
Thereby to see the minutes
how they run,   How many
make the hour full complete;
How many hours bring about the
day;   How many days will
finish up the year;   How many
years a mortal man may live.
When this is known, then to
divide the times: So many
hours must I tend my flock;

So many hours
must I take my rest;
So many hours must I
contemplate; So many
hours must I sport myself;
So many days my ewes have
been with young; so many
weeks ere the poor fools will
ean; So many years ere I
shall shear the fleece: So
minutes, hours, days, months,
and years, Pass'd over to
the end they were created,
Would bring white hairs
unto a quiet grave.
Henry VI, Part 3 -Act II -Sc 5

Therefore doth heaven divide
The state of man in divers functions,
Setting endeavour in continual motion;
To which is fixed, as an aim or butt,
Obedience: for so work the honey-bees,
Creatures that by a rule in nature teach
The act of order to a peopled kingdom.
They have a king and officers of sorts;
Where some, like magistrates, correct at
                                        home,
Others, like merchants, venture trade abroad,
Others, like soldiers, armed in their stings,
Make boot upon the summer's velvet buds;
Which pillage they with merry march
                                        bring home
To the tent-royal of their emperor:
Who, busied in his majesty, surveys

The singing masons building roofs of gold,
The civil citizens kneading up the honey,
The poor mechanic porters crowding in
Their heavy burdens at his narrow gate,
The sad-ey'd justice, with his surly hum,
Delivering o'er to executors pale
The lazy yawning drone. I this infer;
That many things, having full reference
To one consent, may work contrariously;
As many arrows, loosed several ways,
Fly to one mark; as many ways meet in
                                  one town;
As many fresh streams meet in one salt sea;
As many lines close in the dial's centre;
So may a thousand actions, once afoot,
End in one purpose, and be all well borne
Without defeat.
              Henry V ~Act I. Sc. 2

7

Fairy King, attend, and mark:
I do hear the morning lark.

A Midsummer Night's Dream
Act IV, Sc. 1

But look, the morn in russet
mantle clad,
Walks o'er the dew of
yon high eastern hill...

Hamlet ~ Act I, Sc.1

Full many a glorious morning
have I seen Flatter the mountain-
tops with sovereign eye,
Kissing with golden face the
meadow green, Gilding pale
streams with heavenly alchemy...

Sonnet 33

Puck:
ow now, spirit! whither wander
you?

Fairy:
ver hill, over dale,
Thorough bush, thorough brier
Over park, over pale,
horough flood, thorough fire;
I do wander everywhere,
Swifter than the moon's sphere;
And I serve the fairy queen,
o dew her orbs upon the green.
he cowslips tall her pensioners be:
In their gold coats spots you see;
Those be rubies, fairy favours,
In those freckles live their savours:
must go seek some dewdrops here,
And hang a pearl in every
cowslip's ear...

A Midsummer Night's Dream
Act II Sc 1

9

HARK! HARK! THE LARK

Cymbeline - Act II, Sc. 3

HAIL,
many~coloured messenger,
that ne'er
Dost disobey the wife of Jupiter;
Who with thy saffron wings
upon my flowers
Diffusest honey~drops, refreshing
showers;
And with each end of thy blue bow
dost crown
My bosky acres, and my unshrubb'd down,
Rich scarf to my proud earth; why
hath thy queen
Summon'd me hither to this short~
grass'd green?
Iris: A contract of true love to
celebrate,
And some donation freely to estate
On the bless'd lovers.

The Tempest ~ Act IV, Scene 1

But, soft! what light through
yonder window breaks?
It is the east, and Juliet is the sun!
Arise, fair sun, and kill the
envious moon,
Who is already sick and pale with grief,
That thou her maid art far more fair than she:
Be not her maid, since she is envious;
Her vestal livery is but sick and green,
And none but fools do wear it; cast it off.
It is my lady; O! it is my love:
O! that she knew she were.
She speaks, yet she says nothing: what
of that?
Her eye discourses; I will answer it.
I am too bold, 'tis not to me she speaks:
Two of the fairest stars in all the
heaven,
Having some business, do entreat her
eyes
To twinkle in their spheres till they return.
What if her eyes were there, they in her head?

The brightness of her cheek would shame
those stars
As daylight doth a lamp; her eyes in heaven
Would through the airy region stream so
bright
That birds would sing and think it were
not night.
See! how she leans her cheek upon her hand:
O! that I were a glove upon that hand,
That I might touch that cheek.
Juliet ~ Ay me!
Romeo ~ She speaks:
O! speak again, bright angel; for thou art
As glorious to this night, being o'er my head,
As is a winged messenger of heaven
Unto the white ~ upturned wond'ring
eyes
Of mortals, that fall back to gaze
on him
When he bestrides the lazy ~ pacing
clouds,
And sails upon the bosom of the air.
Romeo and Juliet ~ Act II, Sc 2

SHALL I COMPARE THEE TO A SUMMER'S DAY?

Thou art more lovely and more temperate:
Rough winds do shake the darling buds of May,
And summer's lease hath all too short a date:
Sometimes too hot the eye of heaven shines,
And often is his gold complexion dimm'd:
And every fair from fair sometime declines,
By chance, or nature's changing course untrimm'd;
But thy eternal summer shall not fade,
Nor lose possession of that fair thou ow'st,
Nor shall death brag thou wander'st in his shade,
When in eternal lines to time thou grow'st;
So long as men can breathe, or eyes can see,
So long lives this, and this gives life to thee.

Sonnet 18

ME A WILLOW CABIN AT YOUR GATE,

And call upon my soul within the house;
Write loyal cantons of contemned love,
And sing them loud even in the dead of night;
Holla your name to the reverberate hills,
And make the babbling gossip of the air
Cry out 'Olivia!' O, you should not rest
Between the elements of air and earth,
But you should pity me!

Twelfth Night - Act I, Sc.5

'TIS STRANGE

my Theseus, that these lovers speak of.

Theseus:

More strange than true. I never may believe
These antique fables, nor these fairy toys.
Lovers and madmen have such seething brains,
Such shaping fantasies, that apprehend
More than cool reason ever comprehends.
The lunatic, the lover, and the poet,
Are of imagination all compact.
One sees more devils than vast hell can hold;
That is, the madman. The lover, all as frantic,
Sees Helen's beauty in a brow of Egypt.
The poet's eye, in a fine frenzy rolling,
Doth glance from heaven to earth, from earth
to heaven;
And as imagination bodies forth
The forms of things unknown, the poet's pen
Turns them to shapes, and gives to airy
nothing
A local habitation and a name;
Such tricks hath strong imagination
That, if it would but apprehend some joy,
It comprehends some bringer of that joy;
Or in the night, imagining some fear,
How easy is a bush supposed a bear!

— Act V-Sc1 - A Midsummer Night's Dream

16

GO TO, SIR

Tell me, do you know Madam Silvia?

Speed: She that your worship loves?

Valentine: Why, how know you that I am in love?

Speed: Marry, by these special marks: first, you have learned, like Sir Proteus, to wreathe your arms like a malcontent: to relish a love-song, like a robin-redbreast; to walk alone, like one that had the pestilence; to sigh, like a schoolboy that had lost his ABC; to weep, like a young wench that had buried her grandam; to fast, like one that takes diet; to watch, like one that fears robbing; to speak puling, like a beggar at Hallowmas. You were wont, when you laughed, to crow like a cock; when you walked, to walk like one of the lions; when you fasted, it was presently after dinner; when you looked sadly, it was for want of money: and now you are metamorphosed with a mistress, that, when I look on you, I can hardly think you my master.

Two Gentlemen of Verona - Act II, Sc 1

17

When daffodils begin
to peer, ~
With, hey! the doxy over the dale, ~
Why, then comes in the sweet o' the year,
For the red blood reigns in the winter's pale.

The white sheet bleaching on the hedge, ~
With, hey! the sweet birds, O, how they sing! ~
Doth set my pugging tooth on edge;
For a quart of ale is a dish for a king.

The lark, that tirra ~ lirra chants, ~
With, hey! with, hey! the thrush and the jay, ~
Are summer songs for me and my aunts,
While we lie tumbling in
the hay.

The Winter's Tale
Act IV - Sc 2

WELCOME, wanderer. Hast thou
　　the flower there?
Puck. Ay, there it is.
Oberon. I pray thee, give it me.
　I know a bank where the wild thyme blows,
Where oxlips and the nodding violet grows,
　Quite over~canopied with luscious woodbine,
With sweet musk~roses, and with eglantine:
　There sleeps Titania sometime of the night,
Lulled in these flowers with dances and delight;
And there the snake throws her enamelled skin,
Weed wide enough to wrap a fairy in.
And with the juice of this I'll streak her eyes,
And make her full of hateful fantasies.
　Take thou some of it, and seek
　　through this grove:
　　A sweet Athenian lady is in love
With a disdainful youth; anoint his eyes ~
But do it when the next thing he espies
May be the lady. Thou shalt know the man
By the Athenian garments he hath on.
Effect it with some care, that he may prove
More fond on her than she upon her love.
And look thou meet me ere the first cock crow.
Puck. Fear not, my lord: your servant shall do so.

A Midsummer Night's Dream ~ Act II, Sc.1

19

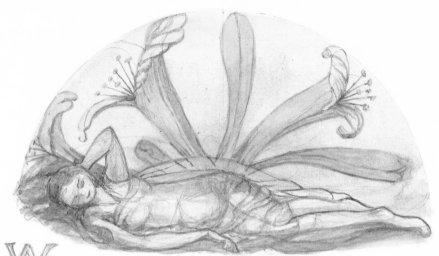

What thou seest when thou dost wake,
Do it for thy true-love take;
Love and languish for his sake:
Be it ounce, or cat or bear,
Pard, or boar with bristled hair,
In thy eye that shall appear
When thou wak'st, it is thy dear,
Wake when some vile thing is near.

Titania awaking:
What angel wakes me from
my flowery bed?...
I pray thee, gentle
mortal, sing
again:

Mine ear is much enamour'd of thy note;
So is mine eye enthralled to thy shape;
And thy fair virtue's force, perforce, doth move me,
On the first view, to say, to swear, I love thee...
...Thou art as wise as thou art beautiful.

Bottom: Not so, neither; but if I had wit enough
to get out of this wood, I have enough to serve
mine own turn.

Titania: Out of this wood do not desire to go:
Thou shalt remain here, whe'r thou wilt or no.
I am a spirit of no common rate;
The summer still doth tend upon my state;
And I do love thee: therefore, go with me;
I'll give thee fairies to attend on thee,
And they shall fetch thee jewels from the deep,
And sing, while thou on pressed flowers do-st **sleep;**
And I will purge thy mortal grossness so
That thou shalt like an airy spirit go.
Pease-blossom! Cobweb! Moth! and Mustard-seed!

Ready.   And I.   And I.   And I.

A Midsummer Night's Dream ~Act II, Sc.2

COME SIT THEE DOWN

upon this flowery bed,
While I thy amiable cheeks do coy,
And stick musk-roses in thy sleek smooth head,
And kiss thy fair large ears, my gentle joy.

Bottom: Where's Pease-blossom?

Pease-blossom: Ready.

Bottom: Scratch my head, Pease-blossom.
Where's Mounsieur Cobweb?

Cobweb: Ready.

Bottom: Mounsieur Cobweb, good mounsieur,
get your weapons in your hand, and kill me
a red-hipped humble-bee on the top of a
thistle; and, good mounsieur, bring me the
honey-bag. Do not fret yourself too much in
the action, mounsieur; and, good mounsieur,
have a care the honey-bag break not; I
would be loath to have you overflown with
a honey-bag, signior. Where's Mounsieur Mustard-
seed?

Mustard-seed: Ready.

Bottom: Give me your neaf, Mounsieur
Mustard-seed. Pray you, leave your curtsy,
good mounsieur.

Mustard-seed: What's your will?

Bottom: Nothing, good mounsieur, but to help Cavalery Cobweb to scratch. I must to the barber's, mounsieur, for methinks I am mar-vellous hairy about the face; and I am such a tender ass, if my hair do but tickle me, I must scratch.

Titania: What, wilt thou hear some music, my sweet love?

Bottom: I have a reasonable good ear in music: let us have the tongs and the bones...

Titania: Sleep thou, and I will wind thee in my arms.

Fairies, be gone, and be all ways away.

Exeunt Fairies

So doth the woodbine the sweet honeysuckle
Gently entwist; the female ivy so
Enrings the barky fingers of the elm.
O! how I love thee; how I dote on thee!

THEY SLEEP

A Midsummer Night's Dream - Act IV, Sc 1

THE CROW

WHEN NEITHER IS ATTENDED,
and I think
THE NIGHTINGALE
if she should sing
by day,
WHEN EVERY
GOOSE is
cackling, would   be thought
No better a   musician
than   the wren.

*How many   things by season season'd
are   to their right praise
and true perfection!
Peace, ho! the moon
sleeps with Endymion,
And would not be awak'd!*

DOTH SING AS SWEETLY AS THE LARK

The Merchant of Venice - Act V, Sc. 1

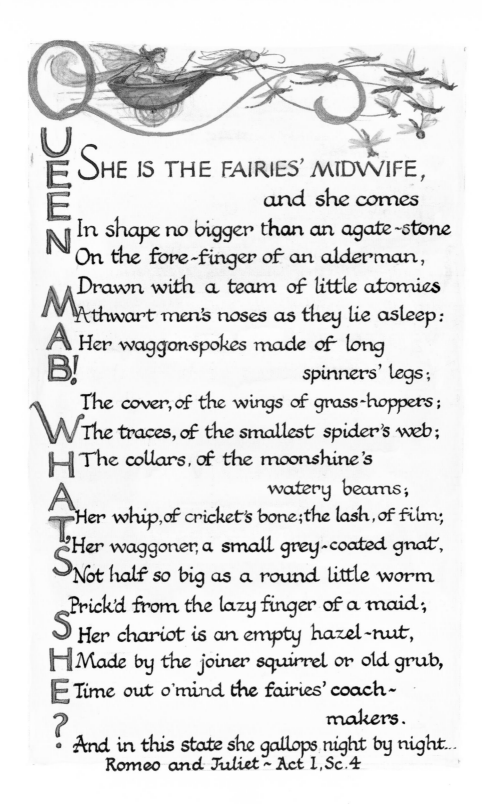

QUEEN MAB! WHATS SHE?

SHE IS THE FAIRIES' MIDWIFE,
and she comes
In shape no bigger than an agate-stone
On the fore-finger of an alderman,
Drawn with a team of little atomies
Athwart men's noses as they lie asleep:
Her waggon-spokes made of long
spinners' legs;
The cover, of the wings of grass-hoppers;
The traces, of the smallest spider's web;
The collars, of the moonshine's
watery beams;
Her whip, of cricket's bone; the lash, of film;
Her waggoner, a small grey-coated gnat,
Not half so big as a round little worm
Prick'd from the lazy finger of a maid;
Her chariot is an empty hazel-nut,
Made by the joiner squirrel or old grub,
Time out o'mind the fairies' coach-
makers.
And in this state she gallops night by night...
Romeo and Juliet ~ Act I, Sc. 4

YOU SPOTTED SNAKES

with double tongue,
Thorny hedgehogs, be not seen;
Newts and blind-worms do no wrong,
Come not near our Fairy Queen.
Philomele, with melody,
Sing in our sweet lullaby,
Lulla, lulla, lullaby,
Lulla, lulla, lullaby,
Never harm,
Nor spell, nor charm,
Come our lovely lady nigh.
So goodnight, with lullaby.

Weaving spiders come not here:
Hence you long-legged spinners, hence:
Beetles black approach not near:
Worm nor snail do no offence.
Philomele, with melody,
Sing in our sweet lullaby,
Lulla, lulla, lullaby,
Lulla, lulla, lullaby,
Never harm,
Nor spell, nor charm,
Come our lovely lady nigh.
So goodnight, with lullaby.

A Midsummer Night's Dream ~ Act II. Sc. 2

Allegro non troppo

p. leggiero

You spot-ted snakes, with dou-ble tongue, Thorn-y hedge-hogs, be not

seen; Newts and blind-worms do no wrong; Come not

cresc.

near our Fai ~ ry Queen

— Newts and blind-worms do no wrong, Come not near our Fai ~ ry

dim.

Queen, Come not near our Fai ~ ry Queen. Hence a~

- way! Hence a ~ way!

— You spot-ted snakes, with dou-ble tongue, Thorn-y

hedge-hogs be not seen. Hence a~

-way! Hence a ~ way!

Hence a — way!

Phil-o-mele with mel - o-dy, Sing in our sweet lull-lul-la-by,

lull-lul-la-by, — lul-la-by — lul-la-by, lul-la-by. Nev-er

harm, Nor spell nor charm, Come our love-ly la-dy nigh.

So, so, good night, so, good night so, good night,

so, so, good night, so good night, with lul-lul-la by, So, good

night, — so, good night, with lull-lul-la-by —

lul - la - by. —

TOIL AND TROUBLE

The influence of the stars, spirits of the dead, sorcery, magic and madness take up this second part. Ulysses speaks of the effect of the stars and Friar Laurence on the power of herbs. Macbeth, urged on by his wife and with ambition inflamed by the prophecies of the three Witches, commits terrible murder and has to suffer the consequences. The spirit of Hamlet's father seeks revenge for his murder, and Puck describes the creatures of the night. Lear contends with the elements and Ariel conjures up the great tempest and shipwreck for his master, Prospero. Sick of the intrigues of court, however, Duke Senior seeks the natural life in the forest of Arden; Ariel sings his last song before being given his freedom by his master and the hallowed time of Christmas holds in check the spirit world.

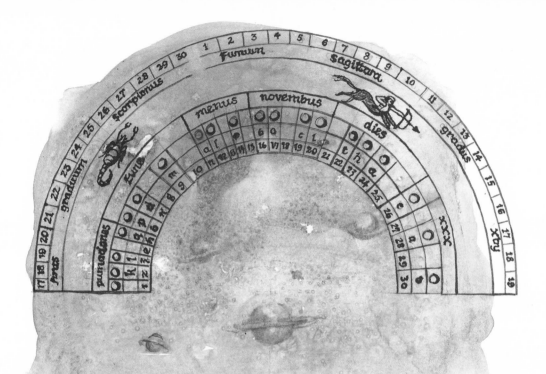

THE HEAVENS
THEMSELVES, THE PLANETS, AND THIS CENTRE

Observe degree, priority, and place,
Insisture, course, proportion, season, form,
Office, and custom, in all line of order;
And therefore is the glorious planet Sol
In noble eminence enthron'd and spher'd

Amidst the other; whose med'cinable eye
Corrects the ill aspects of planets evil,
And posts, like the commandment of a king,
Sans check, to good and bad; but when the planets
In evil mixture to disorder wander,

What plagues, and what portents, what mutiny,
What raging of the sea, shaking of earth,
Commotion in the winds, frights, changes, horrors,
Divert and crack, rend and deracinate
The unity and married calm of states
Quite from their fixure!

Troilus and Cressida ~ Act 1, Sc 3

THE GREY-EY'D MORN
smiles on the frowning night,
Chequering the eastern clouds
with streaks of light,
And flecked darkness like a
drunkard reels
From forth day's path and
Titan's fiery wheels:
Now, ere the sun advance his
burning eye
The day to cheer and night's
dank dew to dry,
I must up-fill this osier cage
of ours
With baleful weeds and precious-
juiced flowers.
The earth that's nature's
mother is her tomb;
What is her burying grave that
is her womb,
And from her womb children
of divers kind
We sucking on her natural
bosom find,

Many for many virtues excellent,
None but for some, and yet all different.
O! MICKLE IS THE POWERFUL GRACE
THAT LIES
IN HERBS, PLANTS, STONES, AND
THEIR TRUE QUALITIES:
For nought so vile that on the earth doth live
But to the earth some special good doth give,
Nor aught so good but strain'd from that fair use
Revolts from true birth, stumbling on abuse:
Virtue itself turns vice, being misapplied,
And vice sometime's by action dignified.
Within the infant rind of this weak flower
POISON hath residence and MEDICINE power:
For this, being smelt, with that part cheers
each part;
Being tasted, slays all senses with the heart.
Two such opposed foes encamp them still.
In man as well as herbs, grace and rude will;
And where the worser is predominant,
Full soon the canker death eats up that
plant.

Romeo and Juliet - Act II, Sc. 3

FIRST WITCH. Thric[e]
cat hath mew'd.
SECOND WITCH.
THIRD WITCH. Harpe[r]
once the hedge~pig
'tis time
FIRST WITCH. Round
cauldron go;
entrails throw. ~ Toa[d]
Days and nights hast thirty~
Boil thou first i' the charmed pot.
ALL. DOUBLE, DOUBLE TOIL AN[D]
SECOND WITCH. FIRE BURN
Eye of newt, and toe of frog,
Adder's fork, and blind~worm's
sting,
For a charm of powerful trouble,
ALL. DOUBLE, DOUBLE
TROUBLE; FIRE BUR[N]
CAULDRON
TROUBLE

DOUBLE, DOUBLE TOIL AND TROUBLE

Macbeth ~ Act IV, Sc. 1

NOW the hungry lion roars,
And the wolf behowls the moon;
Whilst the heavy ploughman snores,
All with weary task fordone.
Now the wasted brands do glow,
Whilst the screech-owl, screeching loud,
Puts the wretch that lies in bed
In remembrance of a shroud.
Now it is the time of night,
That the graves, all gaping wide,
Everyone lets forth his sprite,
In the church-way paths to glide.
And we fairies, that do run
By the triple Hecate's team
From the presence of the sun,
Following darkness like a dream . . .

A Midsummer Night's Dream
Act V, scene 2

36

I am thy father's spirit;
Doom'd for a certain term
to walk the night,
And for the day confin'd
to fast in fires,
Till the foul crimes done in
my days of nature
Are burnt and purg'd away.
But that I am forbid
To tell the secrets of my prison-house,
I could a tale unfold whose lightest word
Would harrow up thy soul, freeze thy young blood,
Make thy two eyes, like stars, start from their spheres,
Thy knotted and combined locks to part,
And each particular hair to stand on end,
Like quills upon the fretful porpentine:
But this eternal blazon must not be
To ears of flesh and blood.
List, list, O list!
If thou didst ever thy dear father love

Hamlet ~ Act I, sc. 5

37

First Witch: Where hast
thou been, sister?
Second Witch: Killing
swine.
Third Witch: Sister,
where thou?
First Witch: A sailor's
wife had chestnuts in
her lap,
And munched, and munched, and munched:
'Give me', quoth I. 'Aroint thee, witch!' the rump-fed
ronyon cries.
Her husband's to Aleppo gone, master o'th' Tiger;
But in a sieve I'll thither sail,
And like a rat without a tail,
I'll do, I'll do, and I'll do.
Second Witch: I'll give thee a wind.
First Witch: Th'art kind.
Third Witch: And I another.
First Witch: I myself have all the other;
And the very ports they blow,
All the quarters that they know
I'th' shipman's card. I will drain him dry as hay;
Sleep shall, neither night nor day
Hang upon his pent-house lid;
He shall live a man forbid:
Weary sev'nights nine times nine
Shall he dwindle, peak, and pine:
Though his bark cannot be lost,
Yet it shall be tempest-tost.

Macbeth—Act I, Sc. 3

38

Where's the King?

Gent: Contending with the fretful elements;
Bids the wind blow the earth into the sea,
Or swell the curled waters 'bove the main,
That things might change or cease;
                    tears his white hair,
Which the impetuous blasts, with eyeless rage,
Catch in their fury, and make nothing of;
Strives in his little world of man to out-storm
The to-and-fro-conflicting wind and rain.
This night, wherein the cub-drawn bear
                    would couch,
The lion and the belly-pinched wolf
Keep their fur dry, unbonneted he runs,
And bids what will take all.

King Lear ~ Act III, Sc. 1

ARIEL:

ALL HAIL, great master,
grave sir, hail: I come
To answer thy best pleasure;
be't to fly,
To swim, to dive into the fire...to ride.
On the curled clouds, to thy
strong bidding task
Ariel, and all his quality.
Prospero: Hast thou, spirit,
Performed to point the tempest
that I bade thee?
ARIEL: To every article...
I boarded the King's ship: now
on the beak,
Now in the waist, the deck, in
every cabin,
I flamed amazement. Sometime
I'ld divide
And burn in many places; on
the topmast,

The yards and bowsprit, would I flame distinctly,
Then meet, and join; Jove's lightning, the precursors
O'th' dreadful thunder-claps, more momentary
And sight-outrunning were not; the fire and cracks
Of sulphurous roaring the most mighty Neptune
Seem to besiege, and make his bold waves tremble,
    Yea, his dread trident shake.
PROSPERO : My brave spirit!
Who was so firm, so constant that this coil
    Would not infect his reason?
ARIEL : Not a soul
But felt a fever of the mad, and played
 Some tricks of desperation; all but mariners
Plunged in the foaming brine, and quit the vessel;
Then all afire with me the king's son Ferdinand,
With hair up-staring – then like reeds, not hair –
Was the first man that leaped;
    cried, 'Hell is empty,
And all the devils are here'.

The Tempest ~ Act I, Sc. 2

COME unto these yellow sands,
And then take hands:
Curtsied when you have, and kissed
The wild waves whist:
Foot it featly here and there,
And sweet sprites bear
The burthen ... Hark! Hark!

Burthen: (dispersedly) Bow~wow!

Ariel: The watchdogs bark:

Burthen: Bow~wow!

Ariel: Hark, hark, I hear
The strain of strutting chanticleer
Cry ~

Burthen: Cockadiddle~dow!

The Tempest ~   Act I, Sc. 2

Full fathoms five thy father lies,
Of his bones are coral made :
Those are pearls that were his eyes.
Nothing of him that doth fade,
But doth suffer a sea-change
Into something rich and strange…
Sea-nymphs hourly ring his knell.
Burthen: Ding-dong.
Ariel: Hark! now I hear them —
Ding-dong bell.

The Tempest - Act I, Sc. 2

First Fisherman: What, ho, Pilch!

Second Fisherman: Ha! come and bring away the nets.

First Fisherman: What, Patch-breech, I say!

Third Fisherman: What say you, master?

First Fisherman: Look how thou stirrest now! come away, or I'll fetch thee with a wannion.

Third Fisherman: Faith, master, I am thinking of the poor men that were cast away before us even now.

First Fisherman: Alas! poor souls; it grieved my heart to hear what pitiful cries they made to us to help them, when, well-a-day, we could scarce help ourselves.

Third Fisherman: Nay, master, said not I as much when I saw the porpus how he bounced and tumbled? they say they're half fish half flesh; a plague on them! they ne'er come but I look to be washed. Master, I marvel how the fishes live in the sea.

First Fisherman: Why, as men do a-land; the great ones eat up the little ones; I can compare our rich misers to nothing so fitly as to a whale;

a' plays and tumbles, driving the poor
fry before him, and at last devours
them all at a mouthful. Such whales have
I heard on o' the land, who never leave
gaping till they've swallowed the whole
parish, church, steeple, bells, and all.
Pericles: (Aside) A pretty moral.
Third Fisherman: But master, if I had been
the sexton, I would have been that day in
the belfry.
Second Fisherman: Why, man?
Third Fisherman: Because he should have
swallowed me too; and when I had been
in his belly, I would have kept such a
jangling of the bells, that he should never
have left till he cast bells, steeple, church
and parish up again.

Pericles –
Act II, Sc.1

45

First Witch. All hail, Macbeth! hail to
thee, thane of Glamis!

Second Witch. All hail, Macbeth! hail
to thee, thane of Cawdor!

Third Witch. All hail, Macbeth! that
shalt be king hereafter.

Macbeth - Act I, Sc. 3

Macbeth...
IS this a dagger which I see before me,
The handle toward my hand? Come, let me
clutch there:
I have thee not, and yet I see thee still.
Art thou not, fatal vision, sensible
To feeling as to sight? or art thou but
A dagger of the mind, a false creation,
Proceeding from the heat-oppressèd brain?
I see thee yet, in form as palpable
As this which now I draw...
...I have done the deed...Didst thou not
hear a noise?
Lady Macbeth. I heard the owl scream and
the crickets cry. Did not you speak?
Macbeth. When?
          Lady Macbeth. Now.
Macbeth. As I descended?
          Lady Macbeth. Ay.
Macbeth. Hark!
Who lies i' the second chamber?
          Lady Macbeth. Donalbain.
Macbeth. This is a sorry sight.

46

Lady Macbeth. A foolish thought to say a sorry sight.

Macbeth. There's one did laugh in's sleep, and one
    cried 'Murder!'
    That they did wake each other: I stood and heard them;
    But they did say their prayers, and address'd them
    Again to sleep.

Lady Macbeth. There are two lodg'd together.

Macbeth. One cried 'God bless us!' and 'Amen' the other:
    As they had seen me with these hangman's hands.
    Listening their fear, I could not say 'Amen',
    When they did say 'God bless us!'

Lady Macbeth. Consider it not so deeply.

Macbeth. But wherefore could I not pronounce 'Amen'?
    I had most need of blessing, and 'Amen'
    Stuck in my throat.

Lady Macbeth. These deeds must not be thought
    After these ways; so, it will make us mad.

Macbeth. Methought I heard a voice cry
                    'Sleep no more!
    Macbeth does murder sleep', the innocent sleep,
    Sleep that knits up the ravell'd sleave of care,
    The death of each day's life, sore labour's bath,
    Balm of hurt minds, great nature's second
                    course,
    Chief nourisher in life's feast, —
                    Macbeth -Act II, Sc.1

47

FAREWELL! A LONG FAREWELL, TO ALL MY GREATNESS! THIS IS THE STATE OF MAN:

Today he puts forth
The tender leaves of hopes; tomorrow blossoms,
And bears his blushing honours thick upon him;
The third day comes a frost, a killing frost;
And, when he thinks, good easy man, full surely
His greatness is a-ripening, nips his root,
And then he falls, as I do. I have ventur'd,
Like little wanton boys that swim on bladders,
This many summers in a sea of glory,
But far beyond my depth: my high-blown pride
At length broke under me, and now has left me,
Weary and old with service, to the mercy
Of a rude stream, that must for ever hide me.

Henry VIII - Act III, Sc.2

48

TOMORROW,
and tomorrow, and tomorrow,
Creeps in this petty pace from day to day,
To the last syllable of recorded time;
And all our yesterdays have lighted fools
The way to dusty death.
OUT, OUT, BRIEF CANDLE!
Life's but a walking shadow, a poor player
That struts and frets his hour upon
the stage,
And then is heard no more: it is a tale
Told by an idiot, full
of sound and fury,
Signifying nothing.

Macbeth - Act V, Sc. 5

49

How use doth breed a habit in a man!
This shadowy desert, unfrequented woods,
I better brook than flourishing peopled towns:
Here can I sit alone, unseen of any,
And to the nightingale's complaining notes
Tune my distresses, and record my woes.

Two Gentlemen of Verona ~
Act V, Sc. 4

Duke S. Now, my co-mates and brothers in exile,
Hath not old custom made this life more sweet
Than that of painted pomp? Are not these
woods
More free from peril than the envious court?
Here feel we but the penalty of Adam,
The seasons' difference; as, the icy fang

And churlish chiding of the winter's wind,
Which, when it bites and blows upon my body,
Even till I shrink with cold, I smile and say
'This is no flattery: these are counsellors
That feelingly persuade me what I am.'
Sweet are the uses of adversity,
Which like the toad, ugly and venomous,
Wears yet a precious jewel in his head;
And this our life exempt from public haunt,
Finds tongues in trees, books in the running brooks,
Sermons in stones, and good in every thing.
I would not change it.

As You Like It - Act II, Sc.2

WHEN ICICLES

hang by the wall
And Dick the Shepherd
blows his nail,
And Tom bears logs into the hall,
And milk comes frozen home in pail;
When blood is nipt, and ways be foul,
Then nightly sings the staring owl

Tuwhit! Tuwhoo! A merry note!
While greasy Joan doth keel the pot.

When all around the wind doth blow,
And coughing drowns the parson's saw,
And birds sit brooding in the snow,
And Marian's nose looks red and raw;
When roasted crabs hiss in the bowl, ~
Then nightly sings the staring owl

Tuwhit! Tuwhoo! A merry note!
While greasy Joan doth keel the pot.
Love's Labour's Lost ~ Act V, Sc. 2

SOME SAY

That ever 'gainst that season comes

Wherein our Saviour's
birth is celebrated,
The bird of dawning singeth
all night long;
And then, they say, no spirit
can walk abroad;
The nights are wholesome;
then no planets strike,
No fairy takes, nor witch
hath power to charm,
So hallow'd and so gracious is the time.

Hamlet ~ Act I, Sc. 1

Under the greenwood tree
Who loves to lie with me,
And turn his merry note
Unto the sweet bird's throat,—
Come hither, come hither, come hither:

Here shall he see
No enemy
But winter and
rough weather.
As You Like It ~

Here shall he see
No enemy
But winter and
rough weather.
Act II, Sc. 5

Who doth ambition shun
And loves to live i' the sun,
Seeking the food he eats,
And pleas'd with what he gets,—
Come hither, come hither,
come hither:

Where
THE BEE SUCKS,
THERE SUCK I.

In a cowslip's bell I lie.

There I couch, when

owls do cry.

On the bat's back I do fly

After summer merrily...

Merrily, merrily, shall I live now,

Under the blossom that

hangs on the bough.

The Tempest ~ Act V, Sc.1

Moderato

Where the
bee sucks there suck I; In a cowslip's bell I _ lie: There I
couch when owls do cry, when owls do cry, when owls do cry. On the
bat's back I _ do _ fly _
_ Af - ter - sum-mer, mer-ri-ly, mer-ri-ly, af _ ter _
sum-mer mer. ri _ ly.
Mer - ri-ly, mer-ri-ly, shall I live
now, Un - der the blos-som that hangs on the bough. Mer-ri-ly _
mer-ri-ly shall I live now, Un - der the blos-som that hangs on the
bough _ Un- der the blos-som that hangs on the bough.

THE PORT OF MARS

The subject of this section is War, and the play of Henry V provides us with the main themes. Calling on a muse of fire the Chorus inspires us to imagine the conflict between France and England. It tells us of the preparations for war and sets the scene of the night before the battle of Agincourt with atmospheric brilliance. There is valour, humour, and rousing words from Henry to inspire his troops before and during battle, and finally victory ascribed to God. After the battle there is the aftermath of destruction and ruin and Burgundy exhorts the enemies to make peace. Time heals the wounds, and Richard of Gloucester describes the transition from war to peace. Finally there is Portia's reminder of the quality of mercy.

This royal throne of kings,
This scepter'd isle, This earth of majesty,
this seat of Mars, This other Eden,
demi- paradise,
This fortress built by Nature
for herself
Against infection
and the hand
OF WAR,

This happy breed of MEN,
This little WORLD,
This precious stone set in the silver sea,

Which serves it in the office of a WALL,
Or as a moat defensive to a house,
Against the envy of less happier lands.

THIS blessed PLOT THIS EARTH

THIS blessed PLOT THIS REALM

THIS IS ENGLAND

Richard II ~ Act II, Sc1

58

I COME NO MORE TO MAKE YOU LAUGH, THINGS NOW

That bear a weighty and a serious brow,
Sad, high, and working, full of state and woe,
Such noble scenes as draw the eye to flow,
We now present. Those that can pity, here
May, if they think it well, let fall a tear;
The subject will deserve it...

Henry VIII ~ Prologue to Act I

ARE NOT YOU MOV'D,

when all the sway of earth
Shakes like a thing unfirm? O Cicero!
I have seen tempests, when the scolding winds
Have riv'd the knotty oaks; and I have seen
The ambitious ocean swell and rage and foam,
To be exalted with the threat'ning clouds:
But never till tonight, never till now,
Did I go through a tempest dropping fire.
Either there is a civil strife in heaven,
Or else the world, too saucy with the gods,
Incenses them to send destruction.

Julius Caesar ~ Act I, Sc. 3

for a Muse of fire, that would ascend
The brightest heaven of invention:
A kingdom for a stage, princes to act,
And monarchs to behold the
                    swelling scene.
Then should the warlike Harry,
                    like himself,
Assume the port of Mars, and at his heels,
Leashed in like hounds, should Famine, Sword, and Fire
Crouch for employment. But pardon, gentles all,
The flat unraisèd spirits that hath dared
On this unworthy scaffold to bring forth
So great an object. Can this cockpit hold
The vasty fields of France? Or may we cram
Within this wooden O the very casques
That did affright the air at Agincourt?
O, pardon! since a crooked figure may
Attest in little place a million;
And let us, ciphers to this great accompt,
On your imaginary forces work ...
Suppose within the girdle of these walls
Are now confined two mighty monarchies,
Whose high uprearèd and abutting fronts
The perilous narrow ocean parts asunder.
Piece out our imperfections with your thoughts:

60

Into a thousand parts divide one man,
And make imaginary puissance.
Think, when we talk of horses, that you see them
Printing their proud hoofs i' th' receiving earth:
For 'tis your thoughts that now must deck our
                                        kings,
Carry them here and there: jumping o'er times;
Turning th' accomplishment of many years
Into an hour-glass: for the which supply,
Admit me Chorus to this history;
Who prologue-like your humble patience pray,
Gently to hear, kindly to judge, our play.
  Henry V   Chorus before Act I

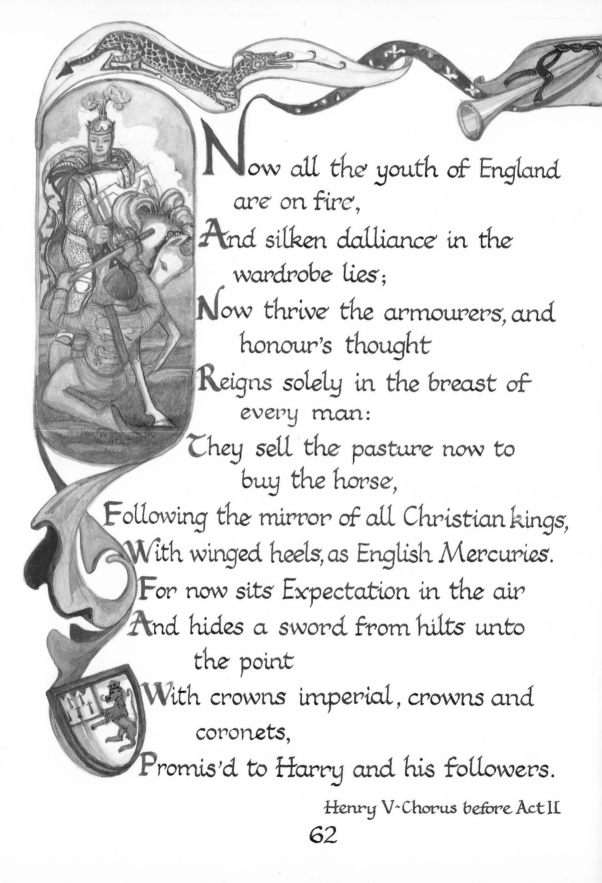

Now all the youth of England
are on fire,
And silken dalliance in the
wardrobe lies;
Now thrive the armourers, and
honour's thought
Reigns solely in the breast of
every man:
They sell the pasture now to
buy the horse,
Following the mirror of all Christian kings,
With winged heels, as English Mercuries.
For now sits Expectation in the air
And hides a sword from hilts unto
the point
With crowns imperial, crowns and
coronets,
Promis'd to Harry and his followers.

Henry V – Chorus before Act II

Where is his son,
The nimble-footed mad-cap Prince of Wales,
And his comrades, that daff'd the world aside,
And bid it pass?

Vernon-All furnished, all in arms,
All plum'd like estridges that wing the wind,
Baited like eagles having lately bath'd,
Glittering in golden coats, like images,
As full of spirit as the month of May,
And gorgeous as the sun at midsummer,
Wanton as youthful goats, wild as young bulls.
I saw young Harry, with his beaver on,
His cushes on his thighs, gallantly arm'd,
Rise from the ground like feather'd Mercury,
And vaulted with such ease into his seat,
As if an angel dropp'd down from the clouds,
To turn and wind a fiery Pegasus
And witch the world with noble horsemanship.

Henry IV, Part I, Act IV, Sc. 2

Launce ~ Nay, 'twill be this hour ere I have done weeping: all the kind of the Launces have this very fault. I have received my proportion, like the prodigious son, and am going with Sir Proteus to the imperial's court. I think Crab my dog be the sourest-natured dog that lives: my mother weeping, my father wailing, my sister crying, our maid howling, our cat wringing her hands, and all our house in a great perplexity, yet did not this cruel-hearted cur shed one tear. He is a stone, a very pebble stone, and has no more pity in him than a dog; a Jew would have wept to have seen our parting: why, my grandam, having no eyes, look you, wept herself blind at my parting. Nay, I'll show you the manner of it. This shoe is my father; no, this left shoe is my father: no, no, this left shoe is my mother; nay, that cannot be so neither: – yes, it is so; it is so; it hath the worser sole. This shoe, with the hole in, is my mother, and this my father. A vengeance on't! there 'tis: now, sir, this staff is my sister; for, look you, she is as white as a lily and as small as a wand: this hat is Nan, our maid: I am the dog; no, the dog is himself, and I am the dog, – O! the dog is me, and I am myself: ay, so, so. Now come I to my father; 'Father, your blessing; now should not the shoe speak a word for weeping: now should I kiss my father; well, he weeps on. Now come I to my mother; O, that she could speak now like a wood woman! Well, I kiss her; why, there't is; here's my mother's breath up and down. Now come I to my sister; mark the moan she makes. Now the dog all this while sheds not a tear nor speaks a word; but see how I lay the dust with my tears.

Two Gentlemen of Verona –
Act II, Sc.3

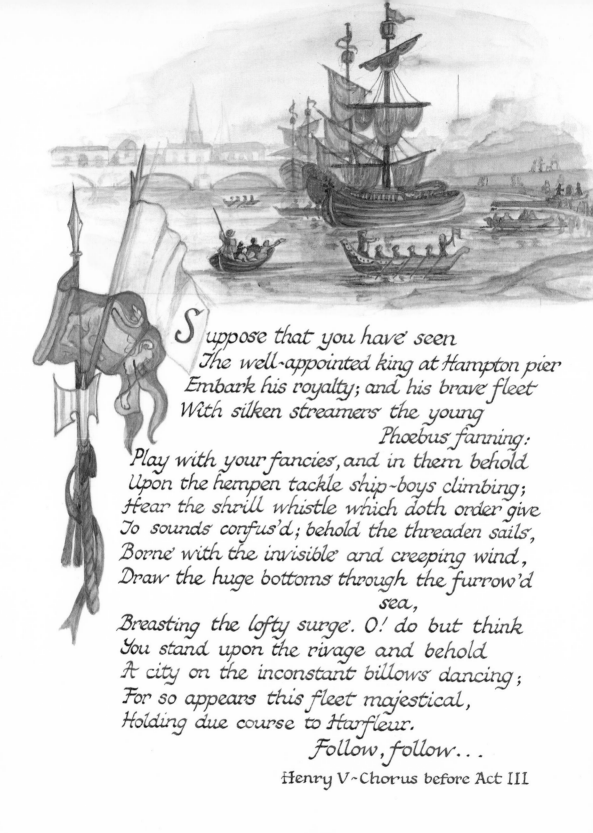

Suppose that you have seen
    The well-appointed king at Hampton pier
Embark his royalty; and his brave fleet
With silken streamers the young
                    Phoebus fanning:
Play with your fancies, and in them behold
Upon the hempen tackle ship-boys climbing;
Hear the shrill whistle which doth order give
To sounds confus'd; behold the threaden sails,
Borne with the invisible and creeping wind,
Draw the huge bottoms through the furrow'd
                    sea,
Breasting the lofty surge. O! do but think
You stand upon the rivage and behold
A city on the inconstant billows dancing;
For so appears this fleet majestical,
Holding due course to Harfleur.
                    Follow, follow…
            Henry V~Chorus before Act III

66

Therefore in fierce tempest is he
coming,
In thunder and in earthquake like a Jove,
That, if requiring fail, he will compel;
And bids you, in the bowels of the Lord,
Deliver up the crown, and to take mercy
On the poor souls for whom this hungry war
Opens his vasty jaws; and on your head
Turning the widows' tears, the orphans' cries,
The dead men's blood, the pining maidens' groans,
For husbands, fathers, and betrothed lovers,
That shall be swallow'd in this controversy.
This is his claim, his threat'ning, and my message;
Unless the Dauphin be in presence here,
To whom expressly I bring greeting too.
French King~For us, we will consider of this further:
Tomorrow shall you bear our full intent
Back to our brother England.

Henry V ~ Act II, Sc. 4

Ambassador~
Your highness, lately sending into France,
Did claim some certain dukedoms, in
                              the right
Of your great predecessor, King
                              Edward the third.
In answer of which claim, the prince our master
Says that you savour too much of your youth,
And bids you be advised there's nought in
                              France
That can be with a nimble galliard won:
You cannot revel into dukedoms there…
He therefore sends you, meeter for your
                              spirit,
This tun of treasure; and in lieu of this,
Desires you let the dukedoms that you claim
Hear no more of you….This the Dauphin speaks.
King Henry~ What treasure, uncle?
Exeter ~   Tennis-balls, my liege.
King Henry~ We are glad the Dauphin is so
                              pleasant with us~
His present and your pains we thank you for:
When we have matched our rackets to these
                              balls,
We will in France, by God's grace, play a set
Shall strike his father's crown into the hazard.
Tell him he hath made a match with such a
                              wrangler
That all the courts of France will be disturbed
With chases…

                    Henry V~Act I, Sc.2

DAUPHIN, I AM BY BIRTH A SHEPHERD'S DAUGHTER

My wit untrain'd in any kind of art.
Heaven and our Lady gracious hath it pleas'd
To shine on my contemptible estate:
Lo! whilst I waited on my tender lambs,
And to sun's parching heat display'd my cheeks,
God's mother deigned to appear to me,
And in a vision full of majesty
Will'd me to leave my base vocation
And free my country of calamity:
Her aid she promis'd and assur'd success;
In complete glory she reveal'd herself;
And, whereas I was black and swart before,
With those clear rays which she infus'd on me,
That beauty am I bless'd with which you see.
Ask me what question thou cans't possible
And I will answer unpremeditated:
My courage try by combat, if thou dar'st,
And thou shalt find that I exceed my sex.
Resolve on this, thou shalt be fortunate
If thou receive me for thy war-like mate.

Henry VI-Part I, Act I, Sc. 2

69

Now entertain conjecture of a time
When creeping murmur and the poring dark
Fills the wide vessel of the universe.
From camp to camp, through the foul womb of
                                    night
The hum of either army stilly sounds,
That the fixed sentinels almost receive
The secret whispers of each other's watch.
Fire answers fire, and through their paly flames
Each battle sees the other's umbered face.
Steed threatens steed, in high and boastful neighs
Piercing the night's dull ear: and from the tents
The armourers, accomplishing the knights,
With busy hammers closing rivets up,
Give dreadful note of preparation.
The country cocks do crow, the clocks do toll,
And the third hour of drowsy morning name.
Proud of their numbers, and secure in soul,
The confident and over-lusty French
Do the low-rated English play at dice;
        And chide the cripple tardy-gaited night,
        Who like a foul and ugly witch doth limp
        So tediously away. The poor condemnéd
        English,
            Like sacrifices, by their
                watchful fires

Sit patiently, and inly ruminate
The morning's danger: and their gesture sad,
Investing lank-lean cheeks, and war-worn coats,
Presenteth them unto the gazing moon
So many horrid ghosts. O now, who will behold
The royal captain of this ruined band
Walking from watch to watch, from tent
                                        to tent,
Let him cry, "Praise and glory on his head!"
For forth he goes, and visits all his host,
Bids them good morrow with a modest smile,
And calls them brothers, friends, and countrymen.
Upon his royal face there is no note,
How dread an army hath enrounded him;
Nor doth he dedicate one jot of colour
Unto the weary and all-watched night:
But freshly looks, and over-bears attaint
With cheerful semblance, and sweet majesty;
That every wretch, pining and pale before,
Beholding him, plucks comfort from his looks.
A largess universal, like the sun,
His liberal eye doth give to every one,
Thawing cold fear, that mean and gentle all
Behold, as may unworthiness define,
A little touch of Harry in the night.

Henry V - Chorus before Act IV

IF WE ARE MARKED TO DIE,
we are enow

To do our country loss: and if to live,
The fewer men, the greater share of honour.
God's will, I pray thee wish not one man more.
By Jove, I am not covetous for gold,
Nor care I who doth feed upon my cost:
It earns me not if men my garments wear;
Such outward things dwell not in my desires.
But if it be a sin to covet honour,
I am the most offending soul alive.
No, faith, my coz, wish not a man from England:
God's peace, I would not lose so great an honour,
As one man more, methinks, would share from me,
For the best hope I have. O, do not wish one more:
Rather proclaim it, Westmoreland, through my
                                    host,
That he which hath no stomach to this fight,
Let him depart, his passport shall be made,
And crowns for convoy put into his purse:
We would not die in that man's company
That fears his fellowship, to die with us.
This day is called the feast of Crispian:
He that outlives this day, and comes safe
                                    home,
Will stand a tiptoe when this day is named,

And rouse him at the name of Crispian.
He that shall see this day, and live old age,
Will yearly on the vigil feast his neighbours,
And say, "Tomorrow is Saint Crispian."
Then will he strip his sleeve, and show his scars,
And say, "These wounds I had on Crispin's day"
Old men forget; yet all shall be forgot,
But he'll remember, with advantages,
What feats he did that day. Then shall our names,
Familiar in his mouth as household words,
Harry the king, Bedford and Exeter,
Warwick and Talbot, Salisbury and Gloucester,
Be in their flowing cups freshly remembered.
This story shall the good man teach his son:
And Crispin Crispian shall ne'er go by,
From this day to the ending of the world,
But we in it shall be remembered;
We few, we happy few, we band of brothers:
For he today that sheds his blood with me
Shall be my brother: be he ne'er so vile,
This day shall gentle his condition.
And gentlemen in England, now a-bed,
Shall think themselves accursed they were not here;
And hold their manhoods cheap, whiles any speaks
THAT FOUGHT WITH US
UPON SAINT CRISPIN'S DAY.

Henry V ~ Act IV, Sc. 3

ONCE more unto the breach,
 dear friends, once more;
 Or close the wall up with our
 English dead…
 In peace, there's nothing so
 becomes a man,
As modest stillness, and humility:
But when the blast of war blows in our ears,
Then imitate the action of the tiger:
Stiffen the sinews, conjure up the blood,
Disguise fair nature with hard-favoured rage:
Then lend the eye a terrible aspect:
Let it pry through the portage of the head,
Like the brass cannon; let the brow o'erwhelm it
As fearfully as doth a gallèd rock
O'erhang and jutty his confounded base,
Swilled with the wild and wasteful ocean.
Now set the teeth, and stretch the nostril wide,
Hold hard the breath, and bend up every spirit
To his full height! On, on, you noblest English,
Whose blood is fet from fathers of war-proof:
Fathers, that like so many Alexanders,
Have in these parts from morn till even fought,
And sheathed their swords for lack of argument.
Dishonour not your mothers: now attest
That those whom you called fathers did beget you!
Be copy now to men of grosser blood,

And teach them how to war! And you, good
yeoman,
Whose limbs were made in England; show us here
The mettle of your pasture: let us swear,
That you are worth your breeding~which I
doubt not:
For there is none of you so mean and base,
That hath not noble lustre in your eyes.
I see you stand like greyhounds in the slips,
Straining upon the start. The game's afoot:
Follow your spirit; and upon this charge,
Cry 'GOD for HARRY, ENGLAND and
SAINT GEORGE!'
Henry V~Act III, Sc.1

This note doth tell me of ten thousand French
That in the field lie slain: of princes in this number,
And nobles bearing banners, there lie dead
One hundred twenty-six: added to these,
Of knights, esquires, and gallant gentlemen,
Eight thousand and four hundred; of the which
Five hundred were but yesterday dubbed knights:...
... O God! thy arm was here;
And not to us, but to thy arm alone,
Ascribe we all. When, without stratagem,
But in plain shock and even play of battle,
Was ever known so great and little loss
On one part and on the other? Take it, God,
For it is none but thine!
Henry V~Act IV, Sc.8

If I demand before this royal view,
What rub or what impediment there is,
Why that the naked, poor, and mangled Peace,
Dear nurse of arts, plenties, and joyful births,
Should not in this best garden of the world,
Our fertile France, put up her lovely visage?
Alas! she hath from France too long been chas'd,
And all her husbandry doth lie on heaps,
Corrupting in its own fertility.
Her vine, the merry cheerer of the heart,
Unpruned dies; her hedges even-pleach'd,
Like prisoners wildly overgrown with hair,
Put forth disorder'd twigs; her fallow leas
The darnel, hemlock and rank fumitory
Doth root upon, while that the coulter rusts
That should deracinate such savagery;
The even mead, that erst brought sweetly forth
The freckled cowslip, burnet, and green clover,

Wanting the scythe, all uncorrected, rank,
Conceives by idleness, and nothing teems
But hateful docks, rough thistles, kecksies, burs,
Losing both beauty and utility;
And as our vineyards, fallows, meads, and hedges,
Defective in their natures, grow to wildness,
Even so our houses and ourselves and children
Have lost, or do not learn for want of time,
The sciences that should become our country,
But grow like savages, ~ as soldiers will,
That nothing do but meditate on blood, ~
To swearing and stern looks, diffus'd attire,
And every thing that seems unnatural.
Which to reduce into our former favour
You are assembled; and my speech entreats
That I may know the let why gentle Peace
Should not expel these inconveniences,
And bless us with her former qualities.
          Henry V ~ Act V, Sc. 2

TIME'S GLORY
is to calm contending kings,

To unmask falsehood, and bring truth to light,
To stamp the seal of time in aged things,
To wake the morn, and sentinel the night,
To wrong the wronger till he render right;
To ruinate proud buildings with thy hours,
And smear with dust their glittering
                              golden towers:

To fill with worm-holes stately monuments,
To feed oblivion with decay of things,
To blot old books, and alter their contents,
To pluck the quills from ancient ravens' wings,
To dry the old oak's sap, and cherish springs;
To spoil antiquities of hammer'd steel,
And turn the giddy round of Fortune's wheel;

To show the beldame daughters of her daughter,
To make the child a man, the man a child,
To slay the tiger that doth live by slaughter,
To tame the unicorn and lion wild,
To mock the subtle, in themselves beguil'd;
To cheer the ploughman with increaseful crops,
And waste huge stones with little water-drops.

The Rape of Lucrece ~ Stanza 135

78

Richard Gloucester:

Now is the winter of our discontent
Made glorious summer by this son of York;
And all the clouds that loured upon our
house
In the deep bosom of the ocean buried.
Now are our brows bound with victorious
wreaths,
Our bruisèd arms hung up for monuments,
Our stern alarums changed to merry
meetings,
Our dreadful marches to delightful
measures.
Grim-visaged war hath smoothed his
wrinkled front...

Richard III ~ Act I, Sc.1

79

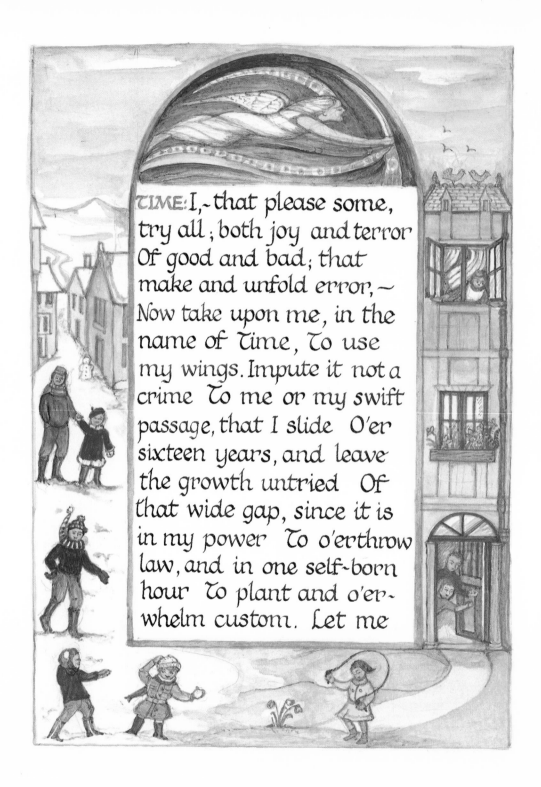

TIME: I,—that please some,
try all; both joy and terror
Of good and bad; that
make and unfold error,—
Now take upon me, in the
name of Time, To use
my wings. Impute it not a
crime To me or my swift
passage, that I slide O'er
sixteen years, and leave
the growth untried Of
that wide gap, since it is
in my power To o'erthrow
law, and in one self-born
hour To plant and o'er-
whelm custom. Let me

80

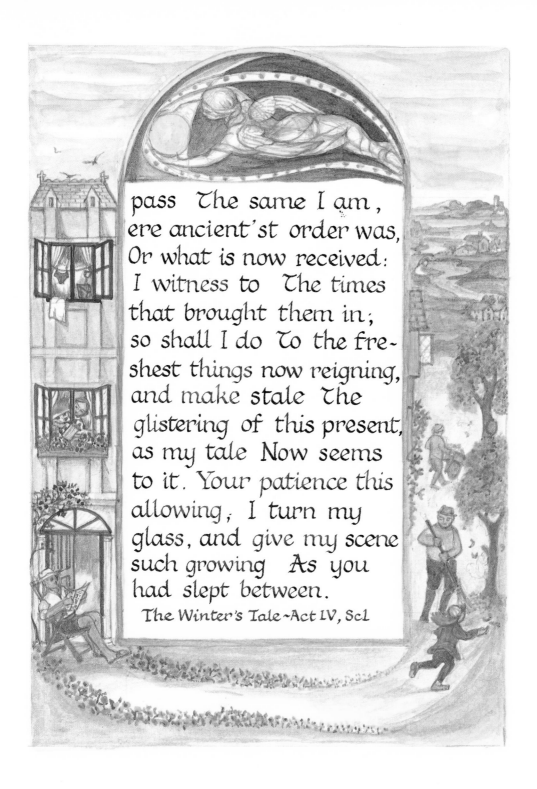

pass The same I am,
ere ancient'st order was,
Or what is now received:
I witness to The times
that brought them in;
so shall I do To the fre-
shest things now reigning,
and make stale The
glistering of this present,
as my tale Now seems
to it. Your patience this
allowing, I turn my
glass, and give my scene
such growing As you
had slept between.

The Winter's Tale ~ Act IV, Sc1

THE QUALITY OF MERCY

is not strained,
It droppeth as the gentle rain from heaven
Upon the place beneath. It is twice blessed:
It blesseth him that gives, and him that takes,
'Tis mightiest in the mightiest, it becomes
The thronéd monarch better than his crown:
His sceptre shows the force of temporal power,
The attribute to awe and majesty,
Wherein doth sit the dread and fear of kings:
But mercy is above this sceptred sway,
It is enthronéd in the hearts of kings,
It is an attribute to God himself;
And earthly power doth then show likest God's,
When mercy seasons justice.

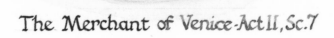

The Merchant of Venice - Act II, Sc. 7

82

WHO CHOOSETH ME

Bassanio chooses the lead casket and hazarding all he has, wins the fair and wealthy lady. The final part of this anthology considers affluence, power and other riches. There is silver and gold and wealth of all kinds: Gremio's possessions, Cleopatra's gorgeous barge, and sumptuous cloth and materials. There is the power of music: Orpheus and his lute, the magic music on Prospero's isle, the music of the spheres, and the effect of music on men and animals. But man is drawn back again to the wealth of the soul. Hamlet describes the greatness of man, Silvia exemplifies the perfect woman, the Sonnet speaks of the marriage of true minds and Hamlet extols the virtue of true friendship. Finally, Prospero reminds us of the ephemeral nature of creation and destroys his staff - the means of his magic art. We are left in the end with Ceres' blessing.

Who chooseth me shall gain what many men desire.

> All that glisters is not gold;
> Often have you heard that told:
> Many a man his life hath sold
> But my outside to behold:
> Gilded tombs do worms infold.
> Had you been as wise as bold,
> Young in limbs, in judgment old,
> Your answer had not been inscroll'd:
> Fare you well; your suit is cold. Act II, Sc. 7

Who chooseth me shall get as much as he deserves.

> The fire seven times tried this:
> Seven times tried that judgment is
> That did never choose amiss.
> Some there be that shadows kiss;
> Such have but a shadow's bliss:
> There be fools alive, I wis,
> Silver'd o'er; and so was this.
> Take what wife you will to bed,
> I will ever be your head:
> So be gone, sir: you are sped. Act II, Sc. 9

84

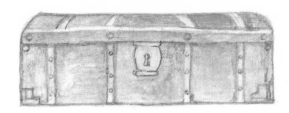

Who chooseth me must give and hazard all he hath.

You that choose not by the view,
Chance as fair and choose as true!
Since this fortune falls to you,
Be content and seek no new.
If you be well pleas'd with this
And hold your fortune for your bliss,
Turn you where your lady is
And claim her with a loving kiss.

Act III, Sc. 2

What find I here?
Fair Portia's counterfeit! What demi~god
Hath come so near creation? Move these eyes?
Or whether, riding on the balls of mine,
Seem they in motion? Here are sever'd lips,
Parted with sugar breath; so sweet a bar
Should sunder such sweet friends. Here, in her
hairs
The painter plays the spider, and hath woven
A golden mesh to entrap the hearts of men
Faster than gnats in cobwebs . . .

Act III, Sc. 2

The Merchant of Venice

85

First, as you know, my house within the city
  Is richly furnished with plate and gold;
Basins, and ewers, to lave her dainty hands;
  My hangings all of Tyrian tapestry:
In ivory coffers I have stuff'd my crowns;
In cypress chests my arras, counterpoints,
  Costly apparel, tents, and canopies,
Fine linen, Turkey cushions boss'd with pearl,
  Valance of Venice gold in needlework,
Pewter and brass, and all things that belong
To house, or housekeeping: then, at my farm,
  I have a hundred milch-kine to the pail,
  Six-score fat oxen standing in my stalls,
And all things answerable to this portion...
  The Taming of the Shrew ~Act II; Sc1

The barge she sat in, like a burnish'd throne,
Burn'd on the water; the poop was beaten gold,
Purple the sails, and so perfumed, that
The winds were lovesick with them, the oars
                                were silver,
Which to the tune of flutes kept stroke, and made
The water which they beat to follow faster,
As amorous of their strokes. For her own person,
It beggar'd all description; she did lie
In her pavilion, ~ cloth ~ of ~ gold of tissue ~,
O'er~picturing that Venus where we see
The fancy outwork nature; on each side her
Stood pretty~dimpled boys, like smiling Cupids,
With divers~colour'd fans, whose wind did seem
To glow the delicate cheeks which they did cool,
And what they undid did.

Antony and Cleopatra ~ Act II, Sc. 2

Lawn as white as driven snow;
Cyprus black as e'er was crow;

Gloves as sweet as damask-roses;
Masks for faces and for noses;

Bugle bracelet, necklace amber,
Perfume for a lady's chamber;

Golden coifs and stomachers,
For my lads to give their dears;

Pins and poking sticks of steel,
What maids lack from head to heel.

Come, buy of me, come; come buy,
                        come buy;
Buy lads, or else your lasses cry;
                        come buy.

The Winter's Tale ~ Act IV, Sc. 3

And now, my honey love,
We will return unto thy father's house;
And revel it as bravely as the best,
With silken coats, and caps, and golden rings
With ruffs, and cuffs, and farthingales, and things;
With scarfs and fans, and double change of
                                    bravery,
With amber bracelets, beads, and all this knavery.
What, hast thou din'd? The tailor stays thy
                                    leisure,
To deck thy body with his ruffling treasure.

O monstrous arrogance!
Thou liest, thou thread, thou thimble,
Thou yard, three-quarters, half-yard, quarter, nail,
Thou flea, thou nit, thou winter cricket thou:
Brav'd in mine own house with a skein of thread!
Away, thou rag, thou quantity, thou remnant;
Or I shall so be-mete thee with thy yard,
As thou shalt think on prating whilst thou
                                    liv'st!
I tell thee, I, that thou hast marr'd her gown.

The Taming of the Shrew ~ Act IV, Sc. 3

... RASCAL THIEVES,

Here's gold. Go suck the subtle blood o' th' grape
Till the high fever seethe your blood to froth,
And so 'scape hanging. Trust not the physician;
His antidotes are poison, and he slays
More than you rob. Take wealth and lives together.
Do villainy; do, since you protest to do't,
Like workmen. I'll example you with thievery.
The sun's a thief, and with his great attraction
Robs the vast sea. The moon's an arrant thief,
And her pale fire she snatches from the sun.
The sea's a thief, whose liquid surge resolves
The moon into salt tears. The earth's a thief
That feeds and breeds by a composture stol'n
From gen'ral excrement. Each thing's a thief.
The laws, your curb and whip, in their rough power
Has unchecked theft. Love not yourselves. Away,
Rob one another. There's more gold. Cut throats;
All that you meet are thieves. To Athens go,
Break open shops; nothing can you steal
But thieves do lose it. Steal no less for this I
                              give you,
And gold confound you howso'er. Amen.

Timon of Athens ~ Act IV, Sc. 3

THE REASON is, your spirits are attentive:
For do but note a wild and wanton herd,
Or race of youthful and unhandled colts,
Fetching mad bounds, bellowing and neighing
                                loud ~

Which is the hot condition of their blood ~
If they but hear perchance a trumpet sound,
Or any air of music touch their ears,
You shall perceive them make a mutual stand,
Their savage eyes turned to a modest gaze
By the sweet power of music: therefore the
                                poet

Did feign that Orpheus drew trees, stones,
                            and floods,
Since nought so stockish, hard, and full of rage,
But music for the time doth change his nature.
The man that hath no music in himself,
Nor is not moved with concord of sweet
                              sounds,
Is fit for treasons, stratagems, and spoils:
The motions of his spirit are dull as night,
And his affections dark as Erebus:
Let no such man be trusted.

               MARK THE MUSIC.

The Merchant of Venice ~ Act V, Sc.1

Be not afeard: the isle is full of noises,

SOUNDS AND SWEET AIRS,

that give delight, and hurt not.
Sometimes a thousand twangling
instruments

Will hum about mine ears; and sometime
voices,

That, if I then had wak'd after long
sleep,

Will make me sleep again: and then,
in dreaming,

The clouds methought would open
and show riches

Ready to drop upon me; that, when
I wak'd

I cried to dream again.

The Tempest ~ Act III, Sc. 2

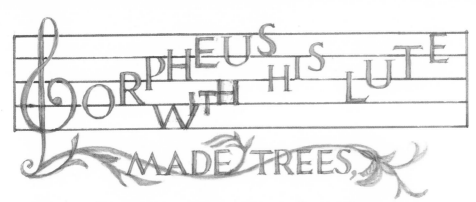

ORPHEUS WITH HIS LUTE

MADE TREES,

And the mountain tops that freeze,
  Bow themselves, when he did sing:
To his music plants and flowers
Ever sprung; as sun and showers
  There had made a lasting spring.

Every thing that heard him play,
  Even the billows of the sea,
Hung their heads, and then lay by.
In sweet music is such art,
  Killing care and grief of heart
    Fall asleep, or hearing, die.

Henry VIII - Act III, Sc. 1

There, my blessing with thee!
And these few precepts in thy memory
Look thou character. Give thy thoughts no tongue,
Nor any unproportion'd thought his act;
Be thou familiar, but by no means vulgar;
The friends thou hast, and their adoption tried,
Grapple them to thy soul with hoops of steel;
But do not dull thy palm with entertainment
Of each new~hatch'd, unfledg'd comrade. Beware
Of entrance to a quarrel, but, being in,
Bear't that th' opposed may beware of thee.
Give every man thine ear, but few thy voice;
Take each man's censure, but reserve thy judgment.
Costly thy habit as thy purse can buy,
But not express'd in fancy; rich, not gaudy;
For the apparel oft proclaims the man,
And they in France of the best rank and station
Are most select and generous, chief in that.
Neither a borrower nor a lender be;
For loan oft loses both itself and friend

And borrowing dulls the edge of husbandry.
THIS ABOVE ALL:
TO THINE OWN SELF BE TRUE,
And it must follow, as the night the day,
Thou canst not then be false to any man.
Farewell; my blessing season this in thee.
Hamlet - Act I, Sc. 3

OUR REMEDIES
oft in ourselves do lie,
Which we ascribe to Heaven: the fated sky
Gives us free scope; only, doth backward pull
Our slow designs, when we ourselves are dull.
All's Well that Ends Well ~ Act I, Sc. 1

I have of late, ~ but wherefore I know not, ~ lost all my mirth, forgone all custom of exercises; and indeed it goes so heavily with my disposition that this goodly frame, the earth, seems to me a sterile promontory; this most excellent canopy, the air, look you, this brave o'erhanging firmament, this majestical roof fretted with golden fire, why, it appears no other thing to me but a foul and pestilent congregation of vapours. What a piece of work is a man! How noble in reason! how infinite in faculty! in form, in moving, how express and admirable! in action how like an angel! in apprehension how like a god! the beauty of the world! the paragon of animals! And yet, to me, what is this quintessence of dust? man delights not me; no, nor woman neither...

Hamlet ~ Act II, Sc. 2

POOR SOUL

THE CENTRE OF MY SINFUL EARTH,
Fool'd by these rebel powers that thee array,
Why dost thou pine within, and suffer dearth,
Painting thy outward walls so costly gay?
Why so large cost, having so short a lease,
Dost thou upon thy fading mansion spend?
Shall worms, inheritors of this excess,
Eat up thy charge? Is this thy body's end?
Then, soul, live thou upon thy servant's loss,
And let that pine to aggravate thy store;
Buy terms divine in selling hours of dross;
Within be fed, without be rich no more:
So shalt thou feed on Death, that feeds on men,

AND, DEATH ONCE DEAD,
THERE'S NO MORE DYING THEN.

Sonnet 146

97

TO ME, FAIR FRIEND,

YOU NEVER CAN BE OLD.

For as you were when first your eye I ey'd,
Such seems your beauty still. Three
winters cold
Have from the forests shook three
summers' pride,
Three beauteous springs to yellow autumn
turn'd
In process of the seasons have I seen,
Three April perfumes in three hot Junes
burn'd,
Since first I saw you fresh, which yet
are green.
Ah! yet doth beauty, like a dial-hand,
Steal from his figure, and no pace
perceiv'd;
So your sweet hue, which methinks still
doth stand,
Hath motion, and mine eye may be deceiv'd:
For fear of which, hear this, thou age unbred:
Ere you were born was beauty's summer
dead.

Sonnet 104

FOR THOU HAST BEEN

As one in suff'ring all that suffers nothing,

A man that Fortune's buffets and rewards

Hath ta'en with equal thanks; and blest are those

Whose blood and judgement are so well commingled

That they are not a pipe for Fortune's finger

To sound what stop she please. Give me that man

That is not passion's slave, and I will wear him

In my heart's core, ay, in my heart of heart,

As I do thee.   Hamlet ~ Act III, Sc. 2

I KNOW HIM AS MYSELF,

for from our infancy

We have convers'd and spent our hours together:

And though myself have been an idle truant,

Omitting the sweet benefit of time

To clothe mine age with angel-like perfection,

Yet hath Sir Proteus, for that's his name,

Made use and fair advantage of his days...   Two Gentlemen of Verona ~ Act II, Sc. 4

99

HIS legs bestrid the ocean: his rear'd arm
Crested the world: his voice was propertied
As all the tuned spheres, and that to friends;
But when he meant to quail and shake the orb,
He was as rattling thunder. For his bounty,
There was no winter in't; an autumn 'twas
That grew the more by reaping; his delights
Were dolphin-like; they show'd his back above
The element they liv'd in: in his livery
Walk'd crowns and crownets; realms and islands were
As plates dropp'd from his pocket.

Antony and Cleopatra - Act V, Sc 2

A woman moved is like a fountain troubled,
Muddied, ill-seeming, thick, bereft of beauty,
And while it is so, none so dry or thirsty
Will deign to sip or touch one drop of it.

100

Thy husband is thy lord, thy life, thy keeper,
Thy head, thy sovereign; one that cares for thee,
And for thy maintenance commits his body
To painful labour, both by sea and land;
To watch the night in storms, the day in cold,
Whilst thou liest warm at home, secure and safe,
And craves no other tribute at thy hands,
But love, fair looks, and true obedience;
Too little payment for so great a debt.
Such duty as the subject owes the prince
Even such a woman oweth to her husband:
And when she is froward, peevish, sullen, sour,
And not obedient to his honest will,
What is she but a foul contending rebel
And graceless traitor to her loving lord?
I am ashamed that women are so simple
To offer war where they should kneel for peace;
Or seek for rule, supremacy, and sway,
When they are bound to serve, love, and obey.
Why are our bodies soft, and weak, and smooth,
Unapt to toil and trouble in the world,
But that our soft conditions and our hearts
Should well agree with our external parts?

The Taming of the Shrew ~Act V, Sc.2

101

SO SWEET A KISS
THE GOLDEN SUN GIVES NOT
To those fresh morning drops
upon the rose,

As thy eye-beams, when their fresh
rays have smote
The night of dew that on my cheeks down flows:
Nor shines the silver moon one half so bright
Through the transparent bosom of the deep,
As doth thy face through tears of mine give light;
Thou shin'st in every tear that I do weep:
No drop but as a coach doth carry thee;
So ridest thou triumphing in my woe.
Do but behold the tears that swell in me,
And they thy glory through my grief will show:
But do not love thyself; then thou wilt keep
My tears for glasses, and still make me weep.
O queen of queens! how far thou dost excel,
No thought can think, no tongue of mortal tell.

Love's Labour's Lost ~ Act IV, Sc.3

102

WHO IS SILVIA? WHAT IS SHE?

That all our swains commend her?
  Holy, fair, and wise is she,
The heaven such grace did lend her,
  That she might admired be.

Is she kind as she is fair?
For beauty lives with kindness:
  Love doth to her eyes repair,
  To help him of his blindness;
And being help'd, inhabits there.

Then to Silvia let us sing,
That Silvia is excelling;
She excels each mortal thing,
  Upon the dull earth dwelling:
  To her let us garlands bring.

Two Gentlemen of Verona ~ Act IV, Sc 2.

Lorenzo.

THE MOON SHINES BRIGHT:
in such a night as this,
When the sweet wind did gently kiss the trees
And they did make no noise, in such a night
Troilus methinks mounted the Troyan walls,
And sigh'd his soul toward
the Grecian tents,
Where Cressid lay that night.

Jessica.

IN SUCH A NIGHT
Did Thisbe fearfully o'ertrip
the dew,
And saw the lion's shadow ere
himself,
And ran dismay'd away.

Lorenzo.

IN SUCH A NIGHT
Stood Dido with a willow in
her hand
Upon the wild sea-banks, and waft her
love
To come again to Carthage.

Jessica.

IN SUCH A NIGHT

Medea gather'd the enchanted herbs
That did renew old Æson.

Lorenzo.

IN SUCH A NIGHT

Did Jessica steal from the wealthy Jew,
And with an unthrift love did run from Venice,
As far as Belmont.

Jessica.

IN SUCH A NIGHT

Did young Lorenzo swear he lov'd her well,
Stealing her soul with many vows of faith,
And ne'er a true one.

Lorenzo.

IN SUCH A NIGHT

Did pretty Jessica, like a little shrew,
Slander her love, and he forgave it her.

Jessica.

I would out-night you, did no body come;
But hark! I hear the footing of a man.

The Merchant of Venice ~ Act V, Sc.1

105

HOW SWEET

the moonlight sleeps upon this bank!

Here will we sit and let the sounds of music

Creep in our ears ~ soft stillness and the night

Become the touches of sweet harmony.

Sit, Jessica. Look how the floor of heaven

Is thick inlaid with patens of bright gold.

There's not the smallest orb which thou behold'st

But in his motion like an angel sings,

Still quiring to the young-eyed cherubins;

Such harmony is in immortal souls!

But whilst this muddy vesture of decay

Doth grossly close it in, we cannot hear it.

The Merchant of Venice - Act V, Sc 1

LET ME NOT

to the marriage of true minds
Admit impediments. Love is not love
Which alters when it alteration finds,
Or bends with the remover to remove:
O, no! it is an ever-fixed mark,
That looks on tempests and is never shaken;
It is the star to every wandering bark,
Whose worth's unknown, although his height be taken.
Love's not Time's fool, though rosy lips and cheeks
Within his bending sickle's compass come;
Love alters not with his brief hours and weeks,
But bears it out even to the edge of doom.
If this be error, and upon me prov'd,
I never writ, nor no man ever lov'd.

Sonnet 116 ~

Ye elves of hills, brooks, standing lakes and groves,
And ye, that on the sands with printless foot
Do chase the ebbing Neptune, and do fly him—
When he comes back; you demi~puppets that
By moonshine do the green sour ringlets make,
Whereof the ewe not bites; and you, whose pastime
Is to make midnight mushrooms, that rejoice
To hear the solemn curfew, ~ by whose
aid—
Weak masters though ye be, I have
bedimmed
The noontide sun, called forth the mutinous
winds,
And 'twixt the green sea and the azured vault
Set roaring war: to the dread rattling thunder
Have I given fire, and rifted
Jove's stout oak
With his own bolt:
the strong~based
promontory

Have I made shak
The pine and

To work mine end
This airy charm—
And deeper than did

…nd by the spurs plucked up

…dar: graves at my command

…ave waked their sleepers, op'd,

…and let 'em forth

…by my so potent art.

But this rough magic I here abjure: and, when I have required Some heavenly music ~ which even now I do ~ I'LL BREAK MY STAFF, Bury it certain fathoms in the earth,

…upon their senses, that …is for,

…ver plummet sound

…'LL DROWN MY BOOK.

The Tempest ~ Act V, Sc.1

YOU DO LOOK, MY SON, IN A MOVED SORT,
AS IF YOU WERE DISMAYED:
BE CHEERFUL, SIR,

Our revels now are ended ... These our actors,

As I foretold you, were all spirits, and

Are melted into air, into thin air,

And, like the baseless fabric of this vision,

The cloud~capped towers, the gorgeous palaces,

The solemn temples, the great globe itself,

Yea, all which it inherit, shall dissolve

And, like this insubstantial pageant faded,

Leave not a rack behind: we are such stuff

As dreams are made on; and our little life

Is rounded with a sleep ...

The Tempest ~ Act IV, Sc. 1

IF WE SHADOWS HAVE OFFENDED, THINK BUT THIS, AND ALL IS MENDED,

That you have but slumber'd here
While these visions did appear.
And this weak and idle theme,
No more yielding but a dream,
Gentles, do not reprehend.
If you pardon, we will mend.
And, as I am an honest Puck,
If we have unearnéd luck
Now to 'scape the serpent's tongue,
We will make amends ere long:
Else the Puck a liar call.
So, good night unto you all.
Give me your hands, if we be friends:
And Robin shall restore amends.

A Midsummer Night's Dream ~ Act V, Sc. 2

Oberon:
Through the house give glimmering light
 By the dead and drowsy fire;
 Every elf and fairy sprite
 Hop as light as bird from brier;
 And this ditty after me
 Sing and dance it trippingly.

Now, until the break of day,
Through this house each fairy stray.
To the best bride~bed will we,
Which by us shall blessèd be;
And the issue, there create
Ever shall be fortunate.
So shall all the couples three
Ever true in loving be;
And the blots of Nature's hand
Shall not in their issue stand:
Never mole, hare~lip, nor scar,

A Midsummer Night's Dream ~ Act V, Sc.2

112

Titania:
First, rehearse your song by rote,
To each word a warbling note:
Hand in hand, with fairy grace,
Will we sing, and bless this place.

All the Fairies sing and dance

Nor mark prodigious, such as are
Despiséd in nativity,
Shall upon their children be.
With this field~dew consecrate,
Every fairy take his gait,
And each several chamber bless,
Through this palace, with sweet peace;
And the owner of it blest
Ever shall in safety rest.
            Trip away:
                Make no stay:
                Meet me all by break of day.

113

HONOUR
RICHES,
MARRIAGE-BLESSING,
Long continuance, and increasing,
Hourly joys be still upon you !
Juno sings her blessings on you.
Earth's increase, foison plenty,
Barns and garners never empty,
Vines with clustering bunches growing,
Plants with goodly burthen bowing;
Spring come to you at the farthest
In the very end of harvest !
Scarcity and want shall shun you;
CERES' BLESSING
so is on you.
The Tempest ~ Act IV, Sc 1

INDEX
First Lines, Source and Context

115

116

119

120

121